Inspiring
Women

Every Day

21

July

THE POWER OF
GENTLENESS

....

HANNAH HEATHER

August

TWISTS AND TURNS

....

NICKI COPELAND

MIX
Paper from
responsible sources
FSC® C021017
www.fsc.org

WAVERLEY ABBEY
RESOURCES

Trading name of **CWR**

Hannah Heather

Hannah Heather is a content writer and discipleship director for 24-7 Prayer International. A passionate theologian, Hannah is currently completing her Master of Theology degree at Oxford University. She and her husband are pastors and elders of Emmaus Road Church in Guildford, and parents to daughter, Thea.

Nicki Copeland

Among the hats Nicki wears are those of wife, mum, writer, speaker, and publisher. She is the author of *Losing the Fig Leaf* and *Less than Ordinary?* In her free time, she can invariably be found with a book in one hand and some chocolate in the other. See www.nickicopeland.co.uk for more information.

The Power of Gentleness

HANNAH HEATHER

This month we are exploring the biblical concept of gentleness. As we can see from today's reading, gentleness is a fruit of the Spirit. This means that it is something that should be evident in the life of every Spirit-filled Christian, seeking to live the way that Jesus taught us.

The word 'gentleness' can often be misunderstood to mean timidity, inaction or weakness. However, the biblical concept of gentleness refers to something altogether different. In the Old Testament, we see the rich imagery of a God who, despite being all-powerful, speaks in a quiet, gentle voice to Elijah. The book of Proverbs commends gentleness as a form of powerful, persuasive, wise leadership. In the New Testament, we meet Jesus who is described as 'gentle and humble in heart' (Matt. 11:29), who turns the world upside down whilst maintaining His posture of gentleness. As the Church is born, the mighty apostle Paul again and again instructs the followers of Jesus to pursue gentleness.

The picture that emerges of biblical gentleness is far more transformative and subversive than we often associate with this word. My prayer as we take a deep dive into this beautiful and powerful fruit of the Spirit, is that we might encounter the incredibly powerful gentleness of Jesus and grow to be ever more like Him.

It can be incredibly difficult to maintain a posture of gentleness, particularly as we face challenging circumstances. Today as we start our journey, we rejoice and take comfort in the truth that gentleness is a gift which is given to us by the Holy Spirit.

Galatians 5:22–26

'love, joy, peace, forbearance, kindness, goodness, faithfulness, gentleness… '
(vv22–23)

For prayer and reflection

Thank You, God, for the fruit of the Spirit that is growing in my life. I pray today for an increase in powerful gentleness. Amen.

Gentle **wisdom**

Proverbs 15:1–7

'A gentle answer turns away wrath, but a harsh word stirs up anger.' (v1)

The book of Proverbs is filled with timeless wisdom on how best to live, and our key verse for today is as practical as it is profound. Have you ever been in a situation which feels tense or fraught and you're unsure how best to proceed? It is often the case that making the choice to meet tension with gentleness can actually be a very powerful and strategic way to deal with these situations.

I love the moment in Shakespeare's play *As You Like It* when the character of Duke Senior delivers this powerful line: 'Your gentleness shall force / More than your force move us to gentleness.'* In this strategic wisdom we are reminded once again that gentleness does not imply weakness; rather it is a very powerful force. I've noticed in both my work life and home life, in my profession and my parenting, that responding with gentleness allows us to impart peace and calm where there is difficulty and disorder.

What's amazing about being a follower of Jesus is that we are given not only the strategy for wisdom in these tense situations, but also the tools we need to be able to act powerfully in the moment. Gentleness is a fruit of the Spirit, so as we go through our day and attempt to impart peace in places of tension, we can lean into the Holy Spirit who will fill us with the self-control and gentleness we need to be able to act wisely.

Can you think back to a time when someone's gentleness transformed your attitude or approach? How might your decision to adopt a posture of gentleness impart something of the peace of God to those you encounter today?

For prayer and reflection

Father God, thank You that by Your Spirit I have both the wisdom and the strength to meet tension with gentleness today. Please give me the courage to be gentle. Amen.

*William Shakespeare, *As You Like It*, II vii

Gentle revolution

Proverbs 25:1–15

'Through patience a ruler can be persuaded, and a gentle tongue can break a bone.' (v15)

As we change pace for the weekend, today I'm reflecting on the life of Martin Luther King Jr, a great example of gentleness. A leader in the Civil Rights Movement in America, in the face of tremendous adversity, violence, discrimination and hatred, King advocated non-violent resistance. Defined by his Christian principles of love and gentleness, his subversive leadership was a crucial voice advocating for racial justice. Listen to the power of his gentle resistance: 'We shall match your capacity to inflict suffering by our capacity to endure suffering. We shall meet your physical force with soul force. Do to us what you will. And we shall continue to love you.'*

His language of 'soul force' reflects the profound courage to resist meeting violence with violence, or hatred with anger. In the passage we have read today we see, in Proverbs, the power of patience and gentleness in efforts to bring about social change. Powerful gentleness resists injustice but refuses to stoop to the level of violence or hatred.

Optional further reading

Martin Luther King III and Coretta Scott King, *The Words of Martin Luther King, Jr.*

* K.D. Miller, *Voice of Deliverance: The Language of Martin Luther King, Jr., and Its Sources* (Athens, GA: University of Georgia Press, 1998) p90

Gentle **whispers**

'And after the fire came a gentle whisper.' (v12)

E lijah was a powerful and fiery character who carried significant spiritual authority. Right before the passage we read today, Elijah has a famous showdown with the false prophets of Baal, challenging them to a contest and calling down fire from Heaven to prove that Yahweh was the one true God. He is confident, cocky and courageous.

It is therefore surprising to find Elijah, as we do in today's reading, dejected, terrified and depressed. How will God respond to the mighty prophet who has collapsed and lost his way? He responds with gentleness.

Elijah is shown an almighty display of power: wind, earthquake and fire. But after the show, God Himself turns up and Elijah is met with a gentle whisper. One of the things I love about a God who gently whispers is that a whisper is an invitation to come *close*. It's impossible to hear a whisper from far away! God knows that, more than anything, Elijah needs to feel the gentle presence of God up close.

In this intimate moment we see that true power can manifest in gentleness. And this gentleness was a far more powerful force to restore his hurting soul than any of the more sensational occurrences at God's disposal. The prophet who called down fire needed more than the spectacular: he needed gentleness.

Is there anyone around you who is feeling dejected, deflated or discouraged? What might God want to say to them today? How could we join with the gentle voice of God and bring encouragement and hope to those around us today? As the gentleness of God restored strength and power to Elijah, may our gentleness bring strength to others today.

For prayer and reflection

Thank You that You are a God who gently whispers. Thank You that Your whispers draw me close and restore my hope. Please help me to gently encourage others today. Amen.

The Big Bounce Forwards

The Big Church Read

Bouncing Forwards by Patrick Regan has been chosen for the Big Church Read. Here's what you need to know. The Big Church read is all about journeying through the book with the author, and then meeting in-person or online to talk about what they have read.

After a tough year for the Church, Waverley Abbey Resources are proud to be supporting this fantastic initiative, and we're so pleased that *Bouncing Forwards* has been selected for it. From 8 September, each Wednesday morning for 10 weeks the Big Church Read will release weekly exclusive videos and content from Patrick Regan to enhance your reading experience.

About Bouncing Forwards

We've all faced difficulties over the last year in some shape or form. Often when we go through challenging times, we're told, 'You'll bounce back.' As well-meant as these words area, the tough times we've been through leave us scarred and changed – so why would we want to go back when we've learnt so much? It's time to bounce *forwards* instead.

In *Bouncing Forwards*, Patrick draws on his own journey of making peace with his on-going anxiety, to look honestly and vulnerably at the temptation to wait for the day when all will be well whilst missing out on what's happening in the here and now. Exploring resilience, acceptance and emotional agility, Patrick shows how we can find meaning in some of life's toughest moments and the hope to journey on.

To find out more about Bouncing Forwards and the Big Church Read, and to make use of the **bulk-buy discount**, visit **waverleyabbeyresources.org/bf**

Gentle **power**

2 Samuel
22:29–36

'You have given me the shield of your salvation, and your gentleness made me great.'
(v36, ESVUK)

The context of today's reading is that David has been miraculously rescued from Saul and is singing this song in thanksgiving to the God who has delivered him from his enemies. Throughout the chapter God is seen as mighty, thundering, all-powerful. At one point David even describes Him having smoke come out of His nostrils and fire from His mouth. The line I find most striking, though, in the midst of this picture of the almighty, all-powerful God, is the verse, 'your gentleness made me great'. The Hebrew here is difficult to translate and another interpretation is 'you stoop down to make me great'.

I think what David is trying to convey here is that the power and wonder and majesty of God are all wonderful to behold, but rather than stay at a lofty distance, reigning from on high, God actually stoops down to our level to pick us up and make us great.

There is a kind of power which stands above others, lords it over them and uses that power to crush, dominate, and control others. But there is a different kind of power which bends down to pick people up, gently stooping to make others great. I love the image of the almighty God not only noticing each one of us, but bending down and lifting us up. True power uses gentleness to make others great.

You may not feel particularly powerful today. Perhaps you want to lean into the image of God stooping down to pick you up, rescue you, and make you great. Or perhaps you're aware that you often find yourself in a position of power over others. What would it look like today to use that power to make others around you great?

For prayer and reflection

God, thank You that Your gentleness makes me great. Please help me to be more like You: to stoop down and pick others up rather than wield my power over them. Amen.

Gentle **tenderness**

Isaiah 40:1–15

'He gathers the lambs… close to his heart; he gently leads those that have young.' (v11)

Yesterday we explored the way that God gently stoops from His position of power to make others great. In our reading today, it is once again evident that God's gentleness and power are not contradictory characteristics, but rather equally important elements of His character.

In the space of two verses, we see the wonderful juxtaposition of the sovereign God who comes with power and rules with a 'mighty arm' (v10): and in the following verse, that same mighty arm is carrying His people like lambs, gently leading those who have young. When we think of mighty. all-powerful rulers, the last thing we imagine is that they would be gently carrying vulnerable young lambs in their arms. Such a level of tender, gentle care is expected from an altogether different type of person – a mother perhaps, not a mighty ruler.

Once again, we see in this passage that gentleness is not something which is distinct from or different to power. Perhaps you have had others make you feel less powerful or less important because you have a nurturing personality or are a full-time homemaker. As you look at this picture of God in His tender care, may you recognise today that God not only affirms and created that part of you – that part of you is just like Him!

As you spend time with God now, you may want to take some time to enjoy the tender care that He has for you today. Enjoy His loving, gentle embrace and reflect on the safety of being in His arms. As you go about your day and show tender care to those around you, remember that this is a family trait which you have inherited from your Father God!

For prayer and reflection

God, I rest in the safety and comfort of Your tender care today. Please help me to reflect Your kindness to all those I meet. Amen.

Gentle **rest**

Matthew 11:25–30

'Take my yoke upon you... for I am gentle and humble in heart, and you will find rest for your souls.' (v29)

Today we move from reflecting on the gentleness of God in the Old Testament to the gentleness of Jesus. In this beautiful passage in the book of Matthew, Jesus describes Himself as 'gentle and humble in heart'. What does it mean for His followers that Jesus has a gentle heart? In this passage, His gentleness is expressed as a source of relief for those who are weary and burdened. Jesus invites them to come to Him and find rest in His yoke.

A 'yoke' in Jesus' day was a heavy wooden device that allowed animals to pull machinery. This word was also used to describe the teaching of a rabbi. Because the Torah was very complex and needed to be applied to all sorts of different situations, rabbis would develop a system of interpretation which their followers would adopt and follow, and this was known as their 'yoke'.

Into this context, Jesus offers His yoke; not to those who are seeking to impress, but to those who are weary and burdened. In contrast to the weightiness of some rabbis' interpretation of the Law, Jesus' yoke is easy and light and actually offers rest rather than burden.

The Message Bible translates this beautifully: 'Are you tired? Worn out? Burned out on religion? Come to me. Get away with me and you'll recover your life. I'll show you how to take a real rest. Walk with me and work with me—watch how I do it. Learn the unforced rhythms of grace.'

If you are feeling weary or burdened today, Jesus gently invites you to come to Him and rest. We don't need to strive or perform; we simply need to receive the gift of grace He has given us and live in light of that freedom.

For prayer and reflection

Lord, please would You bring rest where I am weary today. Help me to leave my burdens at Your feet and take a real rest in Your presence. Amen.

Gentle **humility**

Matthew 21:1–11

'They brought the donkey and the colt and placed their cloaks on them for Jesus to sit on.' (v7)

Jesus usually walked everywhere but in today's passage He rides triumphantly into Jerusalem on a borrowed donkey. No royal chariots or heads of state are waiting to welcome Him, but ordinary people are out in multitudes to shout, 'Hosanna to the Son of David!'. Jesus, as the Son of God, deserves to arrive as a king on a stallion. He chooses instead a simple donkey and selects it deliberately to show He is not like opulent, conquering, earthly kings. He is the Servant King, coming in gentle humility to Jerusalem to suffer and die for the sins of the world.

This is not what the people were expecting. They wanted the Romans defeated, and autonomy once more. They wanted a conquering hero; instead, Jesus seeks only the will of His Father and fulfils the prophecy of Zechariah 9:9. He comes gently as a king on a donkey.

Are we like those followers, wanting Jesus to do something spectacular or miraculous to convert our unbelieving friends or family? We desperately want them to believe, right now, but Jesus shows us a new way, a gentle and humble way of winning their souls through our words and our lives. He encourages us to move slowly, carefully, amongst them, just like Jesus rode without hurrying, to allow all who wanted to follow Him.

The religious leaders saw a rabbi riding into Jerusalem on a donkey. They knew the prophecy. Did they think Jesus was 'Messiah'? Did they join with the crowds throwing their clothes at His feet? Their reaction was indignation and assassination. What is our response to the Servant King today? May we lay our all before Him in a royal welcome!

For prayer and reflection

Father, help us to live with gentle humility to win others to Christ. Amen.

Gentle forgiveness

....

Matthew 5:43–48

'But I tell you, love your enemies and pray for those who persecute you' (v44)

Desmond Tutu, former archbishop of Cape Town, and anti-apartheid and human rights activist, is a great example of gentle forgiveness. Despite living through apartheid in South Africa, Tutu stressed non-violent protest and kindness towards others. In Matthew 5 Jesus exhorts us not only to love our neighbours, but to love and pray for our enemies as well. Jesus offers an extraordinary example of this as He prays for His executioners as He hangs from the cross.

This kind of forgiveness may feel too much for us, but psychologists have shown that living this way brings a better quality of life and mental wellbeing; yet unforgiveness can leave us bitter, fearful and trapped. Forgiveness actually allows us to live life to the full (John 10:10).

Tutu writes: 'We are not responsible for what breaks us, but we can be responsible for what puts us back together again.' If you're struggling with unforgiveness, reflect on this advice. It is not your fault that you have been hurt, but you have the power to move on, stepping into life to the full and refusing to allow the pain to hold you captive.

....

Optional further reading

Desmond Tutu and Mpho Tutu, *The Book of Forgiving: The Fourfold Path for Healing Ourselves and Our World*

Gentle **love**

Mary, Martha and Lazarus were close friends of Jesus. They sent for Him when Lazarus first became sick, but Jesus did not go at once. By the time Jesus arrives, it's too late. Can you imagine the disappointment of the sisters? Why did He ignore their request? Lazarus would still be alive. Why did He not come? It is natural to bring our needs to Jesus, but He may surprise us. Faced with the death of Lazarus, and seeing the depth of grief in Mary and Martha, causes Jesus to have a physical outpouring of emotion which demonstrates His gentle love for His friends. *The Message* translation says when He wept, 'a deep anger welled up within him'. Death not only makes us feel sad, it causes anger, which is not a sin but a normal human response when someone dies. Jesus, the Son of God, here demonstrates His complete human and divine natures in one person. He weeps, He feels anger, He prays, and then He resurrects His friend from the dead. Manhood and deity come face to face with Lazarus before a crowd of astonished people.

The friend is alive again because Jesus loves him deeply. Not only that; this resurrection foretells Jesus' own gruesome death and resurrection in a few days' time. Lazarus' body will die again but Jesus' sacrifice brings eternal life to all believers. John 11:25 says, 'I am the resurrection and the life'. This miracle foreshadows that wonderful truth. Jesus' love for Lazarus is the same love He has for you. Lean into that powerfully gentle love today: a love that weeps when we weep, and reverses the very power of death itself in order that we might have life.

John 11:32–44

'Jesus wept. Then the Jews said, "See how he loved him!"' (vv35–36)

For prayer and reflection

Jesus, thank You for Your powerfully gentle love for me which did not rest until it had overturned death itself. Help me love like You today. Amen.

Gentleness versus **thunder**

Luke 9:51–56

'Jesus turned and rebuked them. Then he and his disciples went to another village.' (vv55–56)

J esus is going to Jerusalem and sends disciples to make arrangements. The people in the Samaritan village refuse to host Jesus because of theological differences. Being like this – closed-hearted and refusing to offer hospitality – can often mean we miss out on extraordinary opportunities and even divine encounters.

Enraged, James and John (nicknamed by Jesus, 'The Sons of Thunder') want to call down lightning on the Samaritans. I love that Jesus includes people with such fiery temperaments in His band of followers! It gives me hope that even in my worst, most angry moments, Jesus still has room for me in His mission and can shape my passion into something positive.

While feeling indignant on behalf of Jesus is appropriate, their violent response is not, and is a sign that there is something more problematic going on in the hearts of these 'thundery' men. Just before this passage, they had been arguing over who would be the greatest. Pride and self-promotion, rather than service and selflessness, is the focus of their hearts. This overflow of hatred and violence towards the Samaritans is a sign that they haven't yet grasped the true power of the kingdom Jesus is inaugurating: one of love and gentle service. When anger overflows quickly and easily in our lives we need to ask ourselves some deeper questions about what might be going in our hearts. Are our responses being shaped by the selfless love and compassion of Jesus or by our own pride and self-promotion? Jesus' firm rebuke is clear. Leading them by example, He brings blessing to a different village; doing good, rather than evil.

For prayer and reflection

Lord, when facing rudeness or rejection, please help me to display gentle patience and love, seeking to bless and not harm others. Amen.

Gentle **waiting**

I n this beautiful parable we see a father who gently waits for the return of one who has wandered far from home. Jesus wants us to catch a glimpse of the gentle compassion of His Father when even *one* sinner turns to Jesus for forgiveness. The father displays love, compassion and pardon when the son does not deserve any of it.

The son's demands for an untimely inheritance were so offensive that the villagers would have stoned him on his return, having so badly dishonoured the father and his village. Instead, in a display of powerful, dangerous gentleness, the father runs to the son before the first stone can be thrown and throws his arms around him, his embrace shielding the son's frail body, making it clear to all that he was dramatically forgiven and welcome.

It can be tremendously difficult to show compassion when we have been hurt by someone. But as we grow closer to Jesus we can pray for the strength to be like the father in this story, extending love, forgiveness and compassion towards others who have hurt us. Here, the father sees the son when he is a long way off and runs to him. Notice that the father was watching and waiting for his boy to come back. He had not given up on him and neither will our heavenly Father stop waiting and watching for the lost.

Have you stopped praying for someone because they seem a long way off? Remember today, as you pray for your loved one, that we are not the only ones waiting: we remember that He is the waiting Father, His eyes on the horizon, just like ours; watching, waiting, hoping for their return home.

Luke 15:11–24

'While he was still a long way off, his father saw him and was filled with compassion for him' (v20)

For prayer and reflection

Thank You, Lord, for Your incredible compassion and love to sinners. Help me to show love and compassion to those around me today. Amen.

Gentle **mercy**

John 8:1–11

'Let any one of you who is without sin be the first to throw a stone at her.' (v7)

I n today's passage, Jesus is being put to the test. The Pharisees wish to trap Him and force His hand towards violence, but Jesus remains in control, quietly and gently powerful, completely diffusing the situation. I can only imagine the terror, humiliation and trauma of the unnamed woman who has been trapped and dragged into this public, masculine space.

Take a moment to picture her in the centre of this story: ashamed, likely very scantily dressed, and shaking with fear as the mob surrounds her. But despite the drama of her story, the people's attention is on the rabbi in the centre of the Temple courts as He slowly and calmly stoops down and begins to write on the ground. Is He writing her death sentence?

The woman probably can't read but she attempts to read his posture and facial expression. His words are firm but gentle: 'any of you who is without sin be the first to throw a stone'. One by one, everyone leaves. When Jesus stands once more He looks her in the eye: probably the first person to do so since this assault began.

When we feel shame over our sin it can make us afraid and want to hide from God. Yet in this moment, as Jesus gently looks her in the eye, He does not condemn her or increase her feeling of shame. Jesus came to take the punishment for all of our sin so none of us need to carry shame any longer. If there is something that is making you feel distant from God today, read this passage again and look into the eyes of Jesus as He stands, having banished all your accusers, and receive his forgiveness afresh: 'neither do I condemn you'.

For prayer and reflection

God, thank You for Your incredible forgiveness of all my sin and shame. Please help me to look You in the eye today and not to hide in my shame. Amen.

Gentle **strength**

Matthew 12:15–21

'A bruised reed he will not break, and a smouldering wick he will not snuff out' (v20)

Matthew here is quoting Isaiah 42: a famous messianic prophecy that the Jewish people were very familiar with. It is a powerful prophecy, depicting a mighty saviour who will come and save the Jewish people, establishing justice for the nations, opening blind eyes and bringing freedom from captivity. The word 'justice' is mentioned three times in the first four verses of this prophecy and there was a very tangible expectancy that the coming messiah would affect dramatic change to establish justice for His people.

The gentleness of Jesus in the face of such expectation was probably confusing. Disappointing even. He looks so different to what people expected that they eventually turn on and kill Him. What do we do when Jesus' action in our lives does not meet our expectations? We can write Him off like some did, or we can lean deeper into the revelation of who He really is, which promises to be far more revolutionary and infinitely better than we could ever have expected.

It's interesting that the section of the prophecy that Matthew chooses to quote references a particularly gentle aspect of the Messiah. He does not come to 'break' or to 'snuff out' but rather to heal and strengthen hearts, and quietly, gently begin to change the world. Do you feel bruised or broken today? Has life been difficult and left you feeling less like a bright light and more like a smouldering wick? Jesus sees you in your brokenness and promises not to break you or give you too much to bear. Instead, He comes in gentleness, bringing light and life and healing, bringing us back to life in all its fullness.

For prayer and reflection

God, I thank You that You are always better than my very best expectations. I pray today for all who are weary and need Your gentle strength. Amen.

Gentle compassion

....

John 13:1–17

'Now that I, your Lord and Teacher, have washed your feet, you also should wash one another's feet.' (v14)

Mother Teresa spent her life serving those who were poor, sick and cut off from society. Her extraordinary compassion brought dignity, healing and community to many people. Her Christian witness speaks powerfully today in a world characterised by selfish ambition, greed and isolation. Gentle compassion led her to hug and lay hands on people who lacked most other human contact. She brings a crucial reminder of the call on Christians to show compassion and community for those who are alone: 'The greatest disease in the West today is loneliness. We can cure physical diseases with medicine, but the only cure for loneliness, despair, and hopelessness is love.'*

The greatest example of selfless love is Jesus: becoming human, drawing close to humankind, laying on hands to heal people, serving, washing feet, and ultimately giving up His life to bring salvation. His gentle compassion towards us is our motivation and the force which empowers us to serve others. What might gentle compassion look like as you try to bring the love of Jesus to others today?

....

Optional further reading

Mother Teresa, *A Simple Path* (compiled by Lucinda Vardey)

*Mother Theresa, as cited in *A Comprehensive Guide to Rehabilitation of the Older Patient* e-book (Edinburgh: Elsevier Health Sciences, 2020) p413

Gentle **words**

John 4:9–30

'Come, see a man who told me everything I've ever done. Could this be the Messiah?' (v29)

Tired from travelling, Jesus arrives in a Samaritan town called Sychar. In Jesus' day, Jews would never speak to Samaritans so it is a great surprise when Jesus asks this disgraced woman, forced to collect water at the hottest part of the day, to give Him a drink. He asks for something simple so He can give her something infinitely valuable. Jesus crosses cultural boundaries to talk to her. Are we willing to do the same to welcome strangers and outsiders into God's kingdom?

Sometimes unbelievers can be critical when we speak of Jesus, but gentle words work far better than arguments. Jesus demonstrates this when He opens conversation with her, ignoring racial hatred and showing divine insight into her situation. Rather than accuse her of immorality, Jesus gently asks about her husband, which immediately pricks her conscience. He goes on to engage in serious theological discussion at a time when women were not typically invited into such conversations. Jesus' approach shows Him to be one who is gentle but truthful, and the woman opens up to discussion rather than shutting Him out. We can learn a lot by using this gentle approach in our own witness to others.

When the disciples return they are surprised that Jesus is speaking to a Samaritan, so she leaves and asks her people to come and see this man, Jesus. Notice, she is not interested in His followers. It is Jesus who impresses her with His gentle words and Jesus who can win her heart. Even those who appear disinterested may be seeking Christ, so let's be more like Jesus in our interactions with them.

For prayer and reflection

Lord, remove all racial and cultural barriers between me and others by changing my attitude and giving me gentle words to use. Amen.

Gentle **leadership**

'I am the good shepherd. The good shepherd lays down his life for the sheep.' (v11)

J esus' leadership style is very different to what we might expect from the almighty Son of God. He describes Himself as a 'good shepherd': an image that would have been very familiar to His first-century listeners. It's fascinating that Jesus does not compare His leadership style to those of kings, emperors or Caesars. Instead, Jesus chooses the humble image of a shepherd who guides, leads and protects their sheep, offering up their own life to save them. Once again, we see Jesus turn our ideas of power and authority on their head as we watch the most powerful man in the world compare Himself to a simple shepherd. This powerfully gentle leadership style is revolutionary: Jesus is again pointing to the kingdom truth that it is those who serve and offer up themselves to benefit others that are closest to looking like the King of kings Himself.

Jesus describes an intimacy between the shepherd and sheep. They know him, recognise his voice and follow only him. Sometimes it can be difficult to know if we are hearing from God or following in the way He wants us to go. I take such encouragement from this passage: Jesus has more faith in my ability to hear and follow Him than I often have! All we need to do is stay close to Jesus and keep our hearts attentive to His voice, and Jesus promises to be our guide, protector and Saviour.

As we think about the gentle leadership of Jesus today, are we following the commands of our shepherd so we do not lose our way? Do we listen to His voice for guidance? Psalm 23:1: 'The Lord is my shepherd, I lack nothing.'

For prayer and reflection

Jesus, thank You that You trust my ability to hear Your voice. Help me stay close to You today and open my ears to hear Your Word. Amen.

Gentle **mercy** – again

Luke 22:39–53

'But Jesus answered,
"No more of this!"
And he touched
the man's ear and
healed him.' (v51)

W hat do those in power want most? Obedience and submission at any cost? Caiaphas, the High Priest in Jerusalem, enters the Jewish world-stage as the one who plots to kill Jesus. He sends a man called Malchus (whose name means 'king') to bring the King of kings to a sham of a trial, leading to His death sentence.

Malchus comes with Judas and a crowd of armed men into the Garden of Gethsemane. The contrast is stark. A quiet, holy place where an unarmed Jesus is praying; the silence assaulted by a noisy, violent rabble. Judas quietly identifies Jesus for Malchus before mayhem ensues and the armed crowd pulls Jesus away from His friends.

This is Malchus' moment in history. One of Jesus' followers leaps forward and cuts off Malchus' ear with a sword. In this chaotic and violent situation, Jesus steps forward calmly, completely in control, and in the most shockingly gentle way demonstrates mercy by touching Malchus' ear and healing him. This is a complete reversal of the power sought and held by people like Caiaphas. It is totally counter-intuitive. But Jesus, in the midst of great anguish, still maintains the kingdom principles He's always practised: gentleness and compassion. Can you imagine the effect this had on Malchus? What did his life look like after such an encounter with Jesus?

Jesus is the king who shows us an entirely different way to wield power. What would it look like to follow Jesus' example of gentle mercy in a wounded world today? How can we be powerfully gentle as we seek to serve everyone around us, even those who seem least deserving of our help?

For prayer and reflection

Thank You, Jesus, for Your gentle mercy to us every day. Help us to bring healing to those who need it today. Amen.

Gentle **selflessness**

John 19:25–37

'Jesus saw his mother… and the disciple whom he loved… he said to her, "Woman, here is your son"' (v26)

Jesus loves His mother Mary dearly. As the eldest son, it was also His job to take care of her, particularly as it seems likely that Joseph had died by this point. Mary had visions and prophecies given before and after His birth, but she could never imagine His life ending so quickly or finding herself at the foot of a cross. No mother could envisage this without wanting to run away, but Mary stayed to the end. Simeon says in Luke 2:35, 'A sword will pierce your own soul too'. Having faithfully said 'yes' to mothering this boy who is now a man, Mary must now watch as her son is brutally taken from her.

Jesus is heartbroken to see His mother suffering; He displays remarkable selflessness as, looking down and seeing John, He entrusts His mother into the care of one He loves dearly. John, from that day on, takes Mary into his own home. As a mother I am deeply moved at Jesus' care in this moment of extreme pain. How can we be selfless even when we find ourselves in difficult circumstances?

It is interesting that the only ones near the cross of Jesus, apart from the Roman soldiers, are: His mother, His mother's sister, Mary the wife of Clopas, Mary Magdalene, and the only disciple recorded, John. The other disciples are probably in hiding, afraid they would be arrested too. Jesus' gentle selflessness goes even further. He knows their fears and weaknesses and forgives them. This is absolute selflessness, putting everyone else first whilst doing the will of His Father. What a Saviour we have; what an example to follow to win a lost world and bring all the Father's children back to Him.

For prayer and reflection

Father, help me to look for opportunities to show gentle selflessness as I put others before my own needs. Amen.

WAVERLEY ABBEY TRUST

COLLEGE

RESOURCES

HOUSE

waverleyabbeycollege.ac.uk   waverleyabbeyresources.org   waverleyabbeyhouse.org

Waverley Abbey Trust

We are a charity serving Christians around the world with practical resources and teaching. We support you to grow in your Christian faith, understand the times in which we live, and serve God in every sphere of life.

The three main areas we focus on are:

- **Mental Health and Wellbeing**
- **Leadership**
- **Spiritual Formation**

Gentle **salvation**

Luke 23:26–34

'Jesus said, "Father, forgive them, for they do not know what they are doing." (v34)

We have seen Jesus live, teach and lead in gentleness and now we see Him die, giving up His life to bring salvation to all. Jesus' death is the opposite of everything we have seen portrayed in His character. It is violent, aggressive, cruel and unjust. In the face of such trauma, Jesus remains loving, compassionate and kind to the end. Refusing to fight back, but instead taking a posture of extraordinarily powerful gentleness, Jesus allows Himself to be 'led like a lamb to the slaughter' (Isa. 53:7). He is not overpowered but rather *lays down* His power in order that He might bring salvation to humankind.

One of the most extraordinary moments on the cross is when Jesus, despite the immense pain He is experiencing, looks up to heaven and asks God to forgive His executioners. I find it hard to imagine the incredible power of forgiveness Jesus demonstrated in that moment. Yet as His followers, seeking now to live like Him, the calling on each one of us is to be bringers of extravagant kindness, compassion and forgiveness. Who might I offer unexpected, extraordinary kindness or compassion to today?

The place where Jesus was killed is called Golgotha, meaning 'the Skull', and at the hour of His death a great darkness descends upon the earth. Through this darkness, the 'light of the world' (John 8:12) begins to shine, bringing hope, life and resurrection for all who follow Him. In the same way, we are now called to let His light shine through our lives. As you think about the dark places in your world today, how might you be a bringer of light and hope in the midst of darkness?

For prayer and reflection

Jesus, thank You for saving me through Your death and resurrection. Please help me bring light into the darkness today. Amen.

Gentle resilience

....

Romans 5:1–11

'we know that suffering produces perseverance; perseverance, character; and character, hope.' (vv34)

Today we reflect on the extraordinarily gentle resilience of Corrie ten Boom: a Christian at the time of the Second World War whose family helped many Jews escape the Holocaust by hiding them in their home. When caught, Corrie and her sister Betsie were sent to Ravensbruck concentration camp. Betsie would never make it out of the camp: before she died, but she told Corrie, 'There is no pit so deep that He [God] is not deeper still'.*

In today's passage, Paul encourages us that suffering need not lead to despair but rather to perseverance, character and hope. We can have hope today, no matter what circumstances we are facing, because we're not alone in our suffering: we are filled with the Spirit who strengthens us.

Corrie also reminds us of the importance of caring for others, even if it costs us. Are our lives truly poured out on behalf of others? No matter what we face today, God's grace is sufficient: not just for us but for those around us as we live lives of gentle resilience, trusting in the Spirit of God who brings us all hope.

....

Optional further reading

Corrie ten Boom, *The Hiding Place*

*Corrie ten Boom, *The Hiding Place* (Peabody, MA: Hendrickson, 2009), p240

Gentle **fruit**

**Galatians
5:19–26**

'love, joy, peace,
forbearance,
kindness, goodness,
faithfulness,
gentleness…'
(vv22–23)

Today we move from our reflections on the gentleness of Jesus to gentleness in the Early Church. When I think of someone like the apostle Paul, gentleness is not the first word I'd use to describe him; but he talked about it a lot! When the New Testament writers refer to gentleness it is clear that they are not speaking of timidity or passiveness, but rather of the powerful kind of gentleness that Jesus demonstrated. As St Francis de Sales says: 'Nothing is so strong as gentleness, nothing so gentle as real strength'.*

Paul describes gentleness as part of the fruit of the Spirit; contrasted with the 'acts of the flesh' (v19) – selfish and sinful attitudes and activities. In other words, the fruit of the Spirit is the natural result of the Spirit present and at work in our lives.

Gentleness can be incredibly challenging. When we face difficult circumstances or frustrating people, gentleness is often the first thing to go; it can be all too easy to give in to our tempers and be short with people or unkind. I find it a huge relief to know that gentle isn't something I have to try and become by myself in my own strength. Instead, I have the power of the Spirit at work in me, making me more and more gentle each day.

One of the ways we can partner with the Spirit's work in producing fruit in our lives is to spend time in prayer and worship. As we draw closer to God, we become increasingly transformed to be like Him. Let's spend some time today in worship and prayer, meditating on the Word of God and asking His Spirit to transform us, growing the gift of gentleness.

**For prayer
and reflection**

**God, thank You
that Your Spirit is
at work in my life,
making me more
like You each day.
Please help me to
grow in the fruit of
the Spirit today.
Amen.**

*J.F. Camus, *The Spirit of S. Francis de Sales, Bishop and Prince of Geneva* (London: Rivingtons, 1872) p13

Gentle **authority**

1 Thessalonians 2:1–12

'Just as a nursing mother cares for her children, so we cared for you.' (vv78)

Just as Jesus handled power radically differently to others around Him, we see Paul modelling a similar approach to leadership here. Paul makes it clear that his status as an apostle granted him the authority to act in a dominant way towards the Church; yet he chooses the way of gentleness, tenderness and compassion. He has learned from Jesus that true power and strength is expressed through service, not dominance. Are you in a leadership position today? What would it look like to choose the less trodden path of servant leadership in your context?

This chapter starts with Paul remembering how he suffered and was treated shamefully in Philippi. However, despite this, he still chooses to come to the churches in Thessalonica in a spirit of gentleness. In fact, some translations say they came as children. These famous apostles choose not to come with demands or seeking praise, not tainted by the rejection they had received, but to come to serve and care for the Church that they loved.

We live in a world where it can be easy to want to protect only our own interests, to seek to come out on top and to always remain in positions of power. And yet the kingdom of God seems to work really differently. Paul has known rejection and yet he is courageous enough to choose gentleness and service. I remember Justin Welby, Archbishop of Canterbury, saying: 'Christians always want to be a bridge, but they rarely are willing to be walked over'. Are there areas in my life where I have been looking to protect myself from rejection instead of having the courage to be gentle?

For prayer and reflection

Thank You that You show me a different way to live; not fearing rejection, but courageously offering gentleness to others, even when my kindness is not returned. Amen.

Clothed with gentleness

**Colossians
3:1–17**

'clothe
yourselves with
compassion,
kindness, humility,
gentleness and
patience.' (v12)

Today's passage shows us how to live with our minds set on heaven and not earth. Paul tells the Colossians that their lives are to be noticeably different to those around them. Now that they have encountered Jesus they can no longer live 'the life [they] once lived' (v7), satisfying their own desires, but must focus on others, dressing for the occasion by 'clothing' themselves in gentleness.

I take solace in the fact that Paul encourages us to 'put on' these things. This suggests to me that there isn't some magic formula that means they are automatically available. That's OK! But just as it isn't OK to walk out of the house before putting on trousers, it isn't OK for the follower of Christ to get out of bed without posturing her heart and attitude into the way of Christ. You might not wake up feeling kind, gentle or compassionate, yet we were never called to live from our feelings – but from our faith. It's not wrong to put it on!

In Romans 13:14, Paul says to 'clothe yourselves with the Lord Jesus Christ'. I think he is expanding on that same idea here. This is what Christ is like: if we want to signpost people to Him, this is how we do it. As D.L. Moody said, 'Out of 100 men, 1 will read the Bible and the other 99 will read the Christian''. As you think about your day and the people around you, what kind of experience will they have when they meet you? Just as our clothes are observed by those we meet, Paul says our gentleness and kindness must be visible and obvious, offering people the opportunity to see Jesus. Take some time now to pray and 'clothe yourself' with Paul's list.

**For prayer
and reflection**

**God, I want to live
differently,
focusing on others
and not myself.
Please clothe me
today in
compassion,
kindness, humility,
gentleness and
patience. Amen.**

'D.L. Moody, as cited by A. McFarland, *10 Answers for Skeptics* (Colorado Springs, CO: Gospel Light, 2011) p37

Gentle **apologetics**

I n today's passage, Peter is talking to a church suffering persecution and abuse for what they believe. Peter encourages them to 'be prepared' to give a reason for why they believe. How do you prepare for difficult conversations? The Bible is clear that being misunderstood and even mocked is part of a Christian's journey. After all, we are called to live in a completely different way because of the hope we have. Therefore, we need to be prepared for when, not if, we find ourselves in difficult conversations. Peter's command is to not just prepare what you say, but how you say it.

As I look around the world today there isn't a lot of gentleness in debate. If anything, social media seems to give people permission to be the opposite. When you're not looking someone in the eye, you're free to be as nasty as you like if you disagree with them. Followers of Jesus have to show a better way. One that matches accusations with compassion and matches attack with respect. We are not called to always agree, but our apologetics cares about tone and not just about truth.

Respect can disagree but still treat the other as human, created in the image and likeness of God. Therefore, we can disagree but should never degrade other people. As you think about difficult conversations with non-Christian family members or friends, what might a gentle answer look like? Just as the quality of gentleness is woven through the fabric of Jesus' life, how could we weave gentleness deeper into the fabric of our conversations, even our disagreements, as we aim for wise, truthful words in a gentle and kind tone.

1 Peter 3:8–22

'answer… everyone who asks you to give the reason for the hope that you have… with gentleness' (v15)

For prayer and reflection

God, please help me to speak not just articulately but kindly when I explain and defend my faith to others. May my gentleness draw people closer to You. Amen.

Pursue gentleness

**1 Timothy
6:11–21**

'pursue
righteousness,
godliness, faith,
love, endurance
and gentleness.'
(v11)

I n this final exhortation from mentor Paul to young
leader Timothy, Paul commends him to pursue
righteousness, godliness, faith, love, endurance
and gentleness. What would it look like to *pursue*
gentleness? How would you make gentleness your goal,
your pursuit, and aim all your efforts at achieving it?

I think it's fascinating that with all the spiritual
language and leadership principles at his disposal, Paul
deliberately chose to end his list with the pursuit of
gentleness. In the Early Church culture, as in ours, this was
not necessarily a principle that was admired, and certainly
not pursued by men such as Timothy who wanted to
achieve great things as leaders. It is counter-cultural,
powerful, upside down living that looks a lot like Jesus.

As we've seen from our reflections on the Old
Testament, the life of Jesus and the Early Church, as well
as of some heroes of the faith, gentleness is a crucial
part of what it means to live, love and lead like Jesus.
Puritan leader, Jonathan Edwards, called gentleness
'the Christian spirit'. Edwards said: 'All who are truly
godly and are real disciples of Christ have a gentle spirit
in them''. As shown by Jesus, this gentle Christian spirit
is deceptively powerful, providing a different way to
wield authority and strength.

**For prayer
and reflection**

**God, thank You for
Your gentleness
and great love for
us. Help us to
pursue You with all
our hearts and
make us more like
You along the way.
Amen.**

Take some time now to reflect on the six characteristics
that Paul lists in this passage and commends Timothy to
pursue. How are you doing on each one? Where might
you need a little work or attention? Today, let's receive
once more the grace of God to run the race set out for us
and pursue the way of gentle Jesus together.

'J. Edwards, *Faith Beyond Feelings* (Colorado Springs, CO: David C. Cook, 2004) p167

Gentle mission

Philippians 4:4–9

'Let your gentleness be evident to all. The Lord is near.' (v5)

We end the month by looking at the life of Jim Elliot. Elliot was a young American missionary to Ecuador in 1956 when he and four companions were killed by the native people group they were attempting to reach with the Gospel. (Their gentle, unarmed approach differed radically from some violent, colonial missionary accounts.) Their deaths were not in vain: the missionary work there continued and thrived after this catalytic moment with many finding faith. Jim's gentleness was evident in his willingness to risk and even give his life for the Gospel cause.

Some years before he was killed, Jim wrote: 'he is no fool who gives what he cannot keep to gain that which he cannot lose'*. It can be difficult to be gentle, especially in the face of those who are not. But as we have seen so powerfully from Jesus, the way of the kingdom is not one of dominance, oppression and superiority; it is one of gentleness, kindness and compassion. As we offer our lives once again today, we remember that whatever we give away, we have a secure inheritance in Jesus as we let our gentleness be evident to *all*.

....

Optional further reading

Elisabeth Elliot, *Shadow of the Almighty: The Life and Testimony of Jim Elliot*

*Jim Elliot, as cited by C.R. Swindoll, *Insights on Matthew 162–8* (Carol Stream, IL: Tyndale House) p40

Become part of someone's testimony

Our Bible reading notes are read by hundreds of thousands of people around the world, and *Inspiring Women Every Day* and *Every Day with Jesus* have recently been made free in the UK. We want everyone, whatever their financial means, to have access to these resources that help them walk each day with our Saviour.

Here's what one *Inspiring Women Every Day* reader wrote to us:

I just wanted to send a message to say how much I've appreciated the most recent readings in IWED. They have been insightful, honest and have deeply touched my needs through the work of the Holy Spirit I know.

As we trust in God's provision, we know there are costs to providing this ministry. Do you have a passion for God's Word changing lives? Could supporting this vision be a way in which you serve?

A gift of just £2 a month from you will put daily Bible reading notes into the hands of at least one person who is hungry to know God and experience His presence every day.

Visit **waverleyabbeyresources.org/donate** to become part of someone's testimony, or use the form at the back of these notes.

Twists and Turns

NICKI COPELAND

Genesis 11:27–32

'Now Sarai was childless because she was not able to conceive.' (v30)

Life has a habit of not turning out quite how we had anticipated, doesn't it? This time last year we were living under the dark shadow of the coronavirus pandemic, and in partial lockdown here in the UK. Life as we had known it had changed, almost beyond recognition for some. Holidays and summer festivals had largely been cancelled, small gatherings were being newly permitted in most areas and face masks had become the latest fashion accessory. We were beginning to adjust to the 'new normal'. The 'new normal' itself, of course, felt as though it was being rewritten day by day. As I write, we have no idea what August 2021 is going to look like, and the past year has very likely been one of significant adjustment and readjustment for all of us.

Sarai found herself in a situation where life hadn't turned out how she had anticipated, either. At that time and in that culture, her inability to conceive and bear children would have been seen as a judgment from God, in addition to being biologically 'faulty'. This would have been the cause of tremendous heartache for Sarai. She would have married Abram many years previously, in the hope and anticipation of bearing a number of children. Sarai would have faced many years of sadness and feeling inadequate, feeling not 'fit for purpose'. How often do we feel that way? How often does life throw us a curve ball that we're not expecting?

Yet, as we will see over the coming weeks, God had a plan for Sarai. It was far beyond anything she would ever have imagined. There were still huge struggles and challenges to be faced, but God's hand was upon her.

For prayer and reflection

Father God, help me to remember, when life doesn't turn out how I'd planned or expected, that Your hand is upon me, and that You have a plan for my life. Amen.

Unbelievable!

Genesis 12:1–3

'I will make you
into a great nation'
(v2)

When was the last time you heard something that you felt was impossible to believe? Perhaps it was that we were going to have a glorious English summer this year (which may or may not have been accurate!). Perhaps you passed a test with flying colours that you weren't even sure you had scraped through.

I studied for a part-time theology degree a few years ago, and when my final result came through, it was better than I had expected. I was genuinely stunned, and kept looking at the result on the portal in disbelief! I was very happy about it, though, and the truth did eventually sink in.

Abram was told by God that he would become 'a great nation'. In order for this to be true, Abram would need to have children — one at the very least. But his wife was unable to... How was that going to work?

Abram was faced with a choice. He could ignore God's words to him, pretend he hadn't heard them and carry on life as before. He could hear God, but interpret God's words in a way that he felt to be consistent with his own situation. He could question God, or even decide not to believe Him and turn away completely. Or — he could choose to believe God, even though he didn't understand how on earth it could be possible that a childless man could be the father of 'a great nation'. He could choose to believe that God, the creator of the heavens and the earth, was bigger than Abram's own circumstances, however cautious and tentative that belief might be.

Can you relate to this? Is there a situation in your life that feels impossible? What might God be saying to you about your situation?

For prayer and reflection

Lord, You know all things, and You are bigger than my circumstances. Help me to trust You with every part of my life — including the seemingly impossible things. Amen.

Why **not** me?

'All peoples on earth will be blessed through you.' (v3)

God had big plans for Abram and Sarai – *really big* plans. Abram must have wondered, 'Why me? Who am I that I should be singled out to become this great nation, and to be a blessing to all the people of the earth? And what does it even mean that "All peoples on earth will be blessed" through me?'

The question Abram could – and perhaps should – have asked is, 'Why *not* me?' And maybe that's a question we, too, should ask ourselves when we think and dream and plan. We have the benefit of the rest of Scripture; we know that God has a habit of choosing the smallest, the youngest, the least significant (humanly speaking), to fulfil His plans: Joseph, Gideon, David, Rahab, Hannah, Mary, among many others.

'Why me?' is a question I have asked myself many, many times in recent years. 'Why would God want to use me through a speaking and teaching ministry? Why would people want to read the things I write? I'm not important enough, wise enough, well known enough, significant enough...'

But perhaps I, too, need to ask, 'Why *not* me?' Perhaps it's because, humanly speaking, I feel so under-equipped to 'do great things for God'. I recognise that any gifts or abilities I have can only have come from Him, and I am completely, utterly dependent on Him when I seek to serve in the ways He has called me to.

So let me ask you: if you could dream big dreams for the kingdom of God, what would you do? Humanly speaking, do you feel that you're too young, too old, too inexperienced, under-qualified...? Even so, instead of asking, 'Why me?' ask, 'Why *not* me?' – and consider what God's answer might be.

For prayer and reflection

What gifts has God given you? How might God want you to use those to bless other people?

Obedience

Genesis
12:1,4–9

'So Abram went, as the LORD had told him' (v4)

The NIV Study Bible tells us that one of the reasons God asked Abram to leave his country, his people and his father's household, is that these three areas are related to deity.* People would worship the gods of their land, of the local culture and of their family. God needed Abram and Sarai to break their ties with the gods of their past so that they could be fully committed to Him.

Abram chose to be obedient to God, even though he had no idea where he was going. And this despite God's promise to him, that he would become a 'great nation'.

I wonder how Sarai might have felt about being uprooted at the age of 65, leaving behind her family, her home, the gods she had always worshipped – everything she had ever known.

New starts aren't easy. Whether it's moving to a new area, starting a new job or college course, moving into a new ministry, or anything else, stepping into the unknown means taking a step of faith. It means leaving certain things behind in order to move forward.

For prayer and reflection

Take some time to pray and reflect on the direction in which God might be leading you, and what He might be asking you to leave behind in order to move forward.

Are you facing new challenges, a new start in any area of your life? Is there something that God is asking you to leave behind so that you can fully step into the new? Are there ties that need to be broken so that you can wholeheartedly embrace what God has planned for you? Perhaps, like Abram and Sarai, God hasn't given you all the details of where you are going and what you will be doing. We step out in faith, holding on to His hand and trusting that He will lead us and guide us along His path. It's not easy, but – as Abram and Sarai would discover – God is faithful, and always keeps His promises.

*NIV Cultural Backgrounds Study Bible (Grand Rapids, MI: Zondervan, 2016), p33

(Dis)honesty

T his is an interesting passage. Abram takes his household to Egypt because there is a severe famine in the land where they have been living. He is clearly worried that, when they get there, the Egyptians will find Sarai desirable, and might then kill Abram to get him out of the way. To protect himself, he instructs Sarai to tell them that she is his sister.

Arguably this isn't Abram's finest moment. He has gone from trusting in God and His promises to taking matters into his own hands to save his own skin. And he displays no regard for the feelings of the other people involved, no thought to how Sarai might be treated in the royal palace. Sadly, this isn't the last time he – and Sarai – will do this, as we will discover as we journey on.

We aren't told how Sarai feels about being passed off as Abram's sister instead of his wife. Does she understand it as a necessary measure in that culture, or is she hurt that Abram is looking after number one and not considering her? She goes along with the deception and doesn't identify herself as Abram's wife when she is taken into the palace (v15), so she displays a level of loyalty to and love for Abram. God has to step in on Sarai's behalf in order for the truth to be exposed.

It can be so easy to view situations through our human eyes, and to take steps to protect ourselves by bending or denying the truth. Fortunately, for Abram and Sarai, the only consequences of their deception are that they have to leave Egypt. But that isn't always the case. Sometimes there are more serious consequences to our dishonesty, for ourselves and for others.

Genesis 12:10–20

'Say you are my sister, so that I will be treated well'
(v13)

For prayer and reflection

Lord, please forgive me for the times when I haven't been completely honest. Please help me to trust You enough to always be truthful. Amen.

Hope and assurance

....

Isaiah 51:1–6

'Listen to me, you who pursue righteousness and who seek the
LORD' (v1)

'Life is hard, but God is good.' Have you ever heard
anyone say that? Perhaps you've said it yourself. It's
good to remind ourselves, when we're facing challenging
situations, that no matter what we are up against, God never
changes. He is always, always faithful, and He always keeps
His promises.

This passage in Isaiah is written to encourage the Israelites
while they are in exile. They have been removed from the
Promised Land, and they have no way of knowing what their
future holds – personally or as a nation.

Through the prophet Isaiah, God offers His people hope.
He tells them that He hasn't forgotten them. He reminds them
of His promise to Abraham, and of the faithfulness He has
shown to all the generations that have gone before. To those
who are faithful to Him, God promises 'joy and gladness…
thanksgiving and the sound of singing' (v3), 'righteousness',
'salvation' and 'justice to the nations' (v5).

And God says, 'my salvation will last forever, my righteousness
will never fail' (v6). No matter what we face in this life, we have
the assurance that God's salvation lasts for ever.

....

Optional further reading

Psalm 105

Covenant

Genesis 15:1–18

'On that day the LORD made a covenant with Abram' (v18)

The concept of covenant was well known in the ancient Near East.* The type of covenant suggested here, between Yahweh and Abram, was like that of suzerain and vassal, a lord and his servant. It was a covenant between two unequal parties – the balance of power rested heavily on the side of one of the parties. Such suzerain/vassal covenants were characterised by authority and protection on the part of the suzerain; and tributes (rather like taxes to be paid), military assistance and exclusive loyalty on the part of the vassal.

The covenant with Abram is one of a number that God makes with His people in the Bible; others being with Adam and Eve, Noah, David; and, of course, the New Covenant that Jesus talks about in Luke 22:20: 'In the same way, after the supper he took the cup, saying, "This cup is the new covenant in my blood, which is poured out for you."'

God didn't need to make a covenant with Abram to prove His commitment; God is faithful to all His promises. But it was a ritual that enabled Abram to understand the seriousness of the pledge he was making. And it is an example of the way God uses traditions and customs that His people are familiar with, to make a point. Abram, of course, would have been fully aware of the meaning of the suzerain/vassal covenant, and he knew he was making a promise to leave behind the gods of his family, his people and his past, and was now pledging his allegiance to Yahweh alone.

Our loving God deserves nothing less than our full commitment. Is there any area of your life where you are holding back from Him?

*I am grateful to Sandra L. Richter for her insights into biblical covenants in *The Epic of Eden* (Downers Grove, IL: InterVarsity Press, 2008), pp72–79

For prayer and reflection

Think about the areas of your life where you struggle to fully surrender to God. Ask Him now for the courage to give everything to Him.

More about covenant

Genesis 15:7–21

'A smoking brazier
with a blazing
torch appeared
and passed
between the pieces'
(v17).

hen they made a covenant, the ancients spoke of 'cutting' a covenant, which comes from the cutting of the animals sacrificed to confirm the agreement. The vassal (the weaker party) would walk between the cut pieces, effectively saying, 'If I don't keep my part of the bargain, may what has happened to these animals happen to me' (see Jer. 34:18).

However, what do we notice in verse 17? Abram has cut the animals in two and has fallen into a deep sleep; and in the darkness a 'blazing torch' appears and moves between the cut pieces. Fire in the Bible is a symbol of the physical presence of God (see, for example, Exod. 3:2; 13:21; 19:18; Acts 2:3). Rather than Abram, the vassal, walking between the cut pieces, it is God, the suzerain, who passes between them. By this action, it is not Abram who is saying, 'May my flesh be torn apart if the covenant is broken', but God.

God never broke His part of the covenant, of course. Abram did indeed have countless descendants and they did take possession of the Promised Land. Yet the covenant *was* broken. And it was God's flesh, through the incarnation of Jesus, that was torn apart as a result.

I am in awe of these hints, even in these early chapters of the Old Testament, of what was to come thousands of years later. I am humbled by God's love for His children so that, even then, He had a plan to rescue humanity, even though we were the ones who were unfaithful – not Him.

**For prayer
and reflection**

**Heavenly Father, I
am in awe of the
way Your plan is
worked out all
through the Bible.
Thank You for Your
incredible love for
me, and for all
Your children.
Amen.**

God needs **help** – or does He?

Yesterday we saw how God demonstrated His commitment to His covenant promises to Abram. Today, we see that, although Abram 'believed the LORD, and he credited it to him as righteousness' (Gen. 15:6), Abram and Sarai are under the impression that God needs a bit of a helping hand to bring about His promise of offspring.

Sarai's infertility is seen as an obstacle to the fulfilment of God's promise. She chooses to offer her slave, Hagar, to Abram to sleep with, in the hope that she will fall pregnant instead. As the child of Sarai's slave, the baby would be considered to be Sarai's.

Such a course of action seems shocking to us in the twenty-first century. But it was not an uncommon practice in the ancient Near East. Fertility and continuation of the family line were considered to be of the utmost importance.

Once again, Abram and Sarai are taking matters into their own hands rather than trusting in God's provision. Perhaps they consider that God's promise is only for Abram, as no mention was made of Sarai. In that case, this would not be seen as unreasonable, bearing in mind the cultural traditions. Sarai acknowledges that Abram needs an heir, and she is unable to provide one; so, humanly speaking, it seems the logical thing to do.

We have the benefit of hindsight, and it is easy for us to judge and criticise Abram and Sarai for their lack of faith (and their treatment of Hagar, but we'll come to that another day). Yet how often do we, too, consider that God needs a bit of help and take matters into our own hands, rather than trusting in Him? Can you think of any examples in your own life?

Genesis 16:1–6

'He slept with Hagar, and she conceived.' (v4)

For prayer and reflection

Loving God, please forgive me for the times when I've taken things into my own hands instead of trusting You. Help me always to have faith in You, in all things. Amen.

Division and **disunity**

Genesis 16:1–6

'Then Sarai ill-treated Hagar; so she fled from her.' (v6)

It's tempting to be critical of Sarai's behaviour in this passage. She has tried to do the right thing by her husband in order to preserve his family line, but the strain is clearly too much for her. She has given Hagar, her slave, to him to produce an heir; but now that Hagar is pregnant, Sarai can't cope. We're told that Hagar begins 'to despise her mistress' (v4). Perhaps she taunts her, or begins to flaunt the fact that she has achieved what Sarai has been unable to do. We don't know. But we do know that it has all become too much for Sarai to bear.

It's a pattern we see all too often. We find ourselves in a difficult situation; we can't cope, so we do something to try to make it better. But then it goes pear-shaped and, instead of taking responsibility for our actions, we blame someone else. This is what Sarai does when she blames Abram for her misery: 'You are responsible for the wrong I am suffering' (v5). Abram isn't prepared to accept the blame, and pushes it back on to Sarai. Consequently, Hagar is so badly treated, she runs away.

Sadly, in all of this, Hagar's feelings are completely overlooked. As a slave, she is considered to be Sarai's possession, and Sarai is free to do as she chooses with her. Yet Hagar is still a human being, made in the image of God, with feelings and thoughts and opinions.

It's easy sometimes to get so caught up in our own problems and challenges that we forget about how other people might be feeling. In our desperation to make our own circumstances better, we don't think about the potential consequences of our actions on those around us.

For prayer and reflection

Lord, please forgive me for the times when I am so focused on myself that I forget about the people around me. Help me to consider their needs and feelings, too. Amen.

No one is excluded

'You are the God who sees me' (v13)

Hagar is desperate. She has been forced to sleep with her mistress's husband and is pregnant with his child, a child who won't even be considered to be hers once he is born. She has unwisely flaunted her pregnancy to her mistress, who is now treating her so badly she would rather throw herself on the mercy of the desert than stay with Sarai.

Hagar is a woman in a staunchly patriarchal society. She is a slave. She is Egyptian – not a part of Abraham's bloodline and therefore not one of God's chosen race. She is unimportant to Abram and Sarai and discarded like a used plaything once she has fulfilled her purpose.

What hope can there be for someone like Hagar?

Hagar doesn't know God, but God knows her. He seeks her out in the desert and reveals Himself to her. Verse 13 is significant: 'She gave this name to the LORD who spoke to her: "You are the God who sees me."' Hagar is the only woman in the Bible privileged to name God. *El-Roi* – 'the God who sees'.

A single, abused, pregnant slave, who has run away because of the desperation of her circumstances, and God appears to her. God sees her and hears her (v11). He knows her circumstances and He understands. And not only does He see and hear and understand, but He also makes Hagar a promise: her descendants 'will be too numerous to count' (v10).

Today, know that God sees you. He sees your circumstances and knows all about them. He hears your cries. No matter who you are or what you might have done, God, *El-Roi*, sees *you* and He hears *you* and He understands *you*. He loves you and He has plans for you. You are safe in His hands.

For prayer and reflection

El-Roi, thank You that You are the God who sees me, hears me and understands me. Thank You that You love me, and that I and my future are safe in Your hands. Amen.

Looking for summer reading? We've got it covered...

Now is the perfect time to explore these books...

Specks and Planks: Stories of Hope, Humility and Humanity

Jeff Lucas

Staying in the Boat: And Other Things I Wish I'd Known

Jeff Lucas

The Dog Who Thought His Name Was No

Judy Moore

Unwavering: The Power of Choice (An Inspiring Women Book)

Jen Baker

Unshakeable Confidence
(An Inspiring Women Book)

Jen Baker

Life Together: The Family Devotional

Steve and Bekah Legg

Cold Cups of Tea and Hiding in the Loo: An Honest Look at Parenting

Annie Wilmot

The Activity Bible (Ages 4–7)

The Activity Bible (Ages 7–11)

To order these titles and dive into your next great read, visit
waverleyabbeyresources.org

Flowers in the wilderness

....

Isaiah 35:1–10

'The desert and the parched land will be glad; the wilderness will rejoice and blossom.' (v1)

We talk sometimes about 'desert experiences', don't we? The desert is considered to be a place of dryness, of hardship and hunger; nothing grows or bears fruit. It's a barren place, where only the strongest and those able to adapt can survive.

Yet, often in the Bible, the desert is a place of preparation, of learning, of pressing in to God and finding new purpose and new paths. When everything else is stripped away, we find ourselves refocusing, reprioritising, and we may well find ourselves stepping out of the desert in a completely new direction.

Hagar met God in the desert. God led the Israelites in the desert (Exod. 13:21–22). David was protected by God in the desert (1 Sam. 23:14). John the Baptist preached in the wilderness, in preparation for the coming Messiah (Matt. 3:1–2). Jesus was led into the desert by the Holy Spirit, where He was tempted by the devil (Matt 4:1–11). This, too, was a time of preparation for His forthcoming ministry.

Are there areas in your life that feel rather like a desert at the moment? What might God be wanting to teach you through these experiences?

....

Optional further reading

Exodus 3:1–10; Matthew 3:1–4:11

What's in a **name**?

Genesis 17:1–7;
15–16

'No longer will you
be called Abram;
your name will be
Abraham' (v5)

D
o you know what your name means? Were you named after a member of your family, or perhaps after someone famous? My forename, apparently, is the female form of Nicholas and means 'victory of the people'.

In the Bible, we are often told the meaning of a person's name. And the name is very often appropriate to the person's character, their vocation or the purpose God has in mind for them. The name Jacob, for example, means 'deceiver'. And indeed, in the early part of his life, he proves to be deceitful. Then God changes his name to Israel, meaning 'he struggles with God'. Jesus, when He meets Simon, calls him Peter (meaning 'rock'), saying, 'On this rock I will build my church' (Matt. 16:18).

In today's passage, God changes Abram's name (meaning 'exalted father') to Abraham (meaning 'father of many'). He also changes Sarai's name to Sarah, which means 'princess'. Very appropriate names, as Abraham and Sarah would become the forefather and mother of the people whom God chose to be a blessing to the whole world. And it's another reminder of God's promise to Abraham that his offspring would be as numerous as the stars in the sky (Gen. 15:5).

If God were to give you a new name today, what might He call you? What element of your personality or your lifestyle might be a suitable description of you? Now, how does this match up with the name you might *want* God to give you? Perhaps you would like to be known as 'Courageous', 'Compassionate' or 'Loving'. Or maybe you would prefer to be known by your vocation: 'Gentle Nurse', 'Wise Teacher', 'Good Mother'. What would you like to be called?

For prayer and reflection

Ask God today to help you live according to the name you would want Him to give you.

God's **promise**

Genesis 17:8–27

'This is my covenant with you and your descendants after you, the covenant you are to keep' (v10)

G od has repeated His promise to Abraham that he will be the 'father of many nations' (v5) and that he and his descendants will live in the land of promise. For God to state His promise once would be enough – God is always faithful to His word – but when He repeats something in the Bible, we know God really means it and wants His people to be in no doubt about it!

This time, God makes it clear to Abraham that His promise will be fulfilled through Sarah: 'I will bless her and will surely give you a son by her' (v16). While Ishmael, who by now is 13 years old, will be blessed with numerous descendants (v20), it is Sarah who will be the 'mother of nations'; it will be Sarah's own son with whom God will establish His covenant (v19).

Abraham and Sarah by this time are 99 and 89 respectively; way too old to be starting a family, humanly speaking. More than 14 years have passed since God promised Abraham that he would have a son, and 24 years since God's first promise to make him 'into a great nation'. Abraham and Sarah could be forgiven for thinking that that boat has long since sailed. But God hasn't forgotten His promise, and the time for its fulfilment is drawing ever nearer.

There are times when we can be tempted to give up when we don't see an immediate answer to our prayers. Perhaps we believe God has given us a clear word about our future, but when it doesn't come to fruition soon, we begin to doubt, thinking we must have misheard or misunderstood. But God doesn't forget – ever.

Let's hang on to God's promises, and trust in His faithfulness and His perfect timing for their fulfilment.

For prayer and reflection

Father God, thank You for Your faithfulness to me. Help me to trust in You and in Your perfect timing for my life. Amen.

Welcome

Genesis 18:1–8

'Let me get you something to eat' (v5)

Hospitality was an important element in ancient Near Eastern culture. Abraham is keen to provide all that his unexpected guests might need: shelter, rest, foot-washing and food. Abraham and Sarah might be going through a bit of a tough time, and are unsure of their own future, but that doesn't stop them fulfilling their cultural obligations and looking after those in need. There is a sense of urgency in verses 6 and 7, conveying Abraham's keenness to serve his visitors: 'hurried'; '"Quick," he said'; 'he ran'; 'hurried' again.

There is mystery in this passage, too. Is Abraham's enthusiasm simply his normal response to company, or does he sense something extra special about these particular guests? The writer to the Hebrews reminds his hearers, 'Do not forget to show hospitality to strangers, for by so doing some people have shown hospitality to angels without knowing it' (Heb. 13:2). Perhaps he has Abraham in mind as he writes this.

Hospitality remains an important ministry, and some are very gifted in this area. There are so many opportunities to serve. We can welcome others into our homes and share a meal together. For various reasons, some people might not be able to do that. But there is still lots we can do: we can donate food to our local food bank; we can buy a sandwich and a hot drink for a homeless person, or seek ways to support a local charity that works with those who are homeless. We can advocate for the needs of poor and marginalised people, both in our own nation and further afield. We can speak out against injustice and lobby our governments to provide for those in need.

For prayer and reflection

Lord, please help me to be as enthusiastic as Abraham about being welcoming and hospitable to others, and to do what I can to meet others' needs. Amen.

The impossible **made possible**

Genesis 18:9–15

'So Sarah laughed to herself' (v12)

Clearly, it is the Lord who visits Abraham and Sarah here, and at long last puts a time frame on the promise of a son to the couple. Sarah's reaction is to laugh at the irony – all these years she has longed for a child of her own. And now that she is well past child-bearing age, can it really be true that, at the age of 90, she will finally have the joy of a child?

Abraham's reaction, back in verse 17 of chapter 17, was also to laugh when God told him that Sarah would be 'the mother of nations'. He, too, finds it hard to believe that his wife, who has so far been unable to have children, will actually give birth to a son.

Perhaps Sarah feels she is being mocked by these visitors. Or perhaps the deep pain of having been childless for so many years means that Sarah doesn't dare to believe that she will experience such a miracle. In that culture, Sarah would feel herself to be valueless, worthless, unable to fulfil her function as a woman and a wife.

God knows the deepest longings of our hearts. Unfulfilled dreams and ambitions can leave deep scars. We might have been so sure that our life was heading in a particular direction, when something happened and we now find ourselves going completely the opposite way. God knows all about it. He knew before it even happened – nothing takes Him by surprise. He has plans for your life – and all His plans are good plans.

God says to you today, 'I love you, and you are very precious to Me. I love you because I created you, not because of the things you can or can't do, or because of the things you have or haven't done. You are My child. Allow Me to love you just as you are.'

For prayer and reflection

'"For I know the plans I have for you," declares the LORD, "plans to prosper you and not to harm you, plans to give you hope and a future"' (Jer. 29:11).

(Dis)honesty (again)

Genesis 20:1–18

'She is my sister.'
(v2)

We humans can be slow to learn at times, can't we? Here we see Abraham and Sarah repeating the mistake they made in chapter 12, when they pretended that Sarah was his sister rather than his wife. Even though she *is* his half-sister, as we are told in verse 12, Abraham's intention is clearly to deceive, to save his own skin once again.

Yet, this time, there is more at stake. Abraham and Sarah have been told that, within the next year, she will become pregnant and give birth to a son, the heir of God's promise. If Abimelek were to sleep with Sarah, there would be a question mark over who the baby's father is, when he is born. This would change the entire course of history. Once again, God intervenes – both to save Abraham and Sarah and to protect their descendants, to whom and through whom He has promised so much.

God is so gracious, and so patient with us. We make the same mistakes time after time, and God continues to forgive us; to pick us up, dust us down and set us back on our feet once again. God's plans – fortunately – will not be thwarted by our mistakes, although, as we have mentioned before, there are always consequences for our actions, whether for ourselves or for other people.

God protected Abraham, Sarah, Isaac and Abimelek from the consequences of Abraham and Sarah's error this time. But sometimes God allows us to experience the consequences. Being a follower of Jesus isn't an insurance policy to do whatever we like in the knowledge that God will sort out any mess we make. We live in His grace, and trust that He will guide us – and we are to be obedient to His guidance.

For prayer and reflection

Lord, please help me to be faithful and obedient to You, even when it's difficult. And please help me to learn from my mistakes. Amen.

Faithful God

....

Psalm 33:1–11

'For the word of the LORD is right and true; he is faithful in all he does.' (v4)

F aithfulness, commitment, loyalty: sadly, these are values that aren't considered to be particularly important by many in western society these days. Our culture tells us that we can and should do whatever we want, if it makes us feel good. It doesn't matter about anyone else – they can look after themselves.

But this is not God's way. God is our role model. He is the one we are to follow. His are the values we are to adopt.

Over the last couple of weeks, we have seen many examples of God's faithfulness to Abraham and Sarah, despite the mistakes they have made along the way. This weekend, let's be encouraged that God is always faithful to His children, no matter what, and that 'the plans of the LORD stand firm for ever, the purposes of his heart through all generations' (v11).

Let's buck the trend and display love, compassion, loyalty, faithfulness, and all the fruit of the Spirit God calls us to bear in our lives. Let us be countercultural, bringing the goodness of God's kingdom to earth.

....

Optional further reading

Psalm 33:12–22; Galatians 5:13–26

Joy and **laughter**

At long, long last, here is the beginning of the fulfilment of God's promise to Abraham and Sarah. The son He has been promising them for many years is finally born. God tells Abraham to give their son the name Isaac, which means 'he laughs'.

As God gives Sarah what she has so longed for, he brings laughter back into her and Abraham's lives. Abraham and Sarah's disbelieving, ironic laughter from chapters 17 and 18 is transformed into true and deep joy.

Abraham is 100 years old when Isaac is born, and Sarah is 90. They have waited a long time for the fulfilment of God's promise. And this is just the beginning – there is so much more to come. Yet they won't see it all. Abraham and Sarah won't live to see the 'great nation' that their descendants will become (Gen. 12:2), nor will they see them take possession of the Promised Land, many generations later.

Sometimes God's promises are much bigger than us and our individual lives. There is always a much bigger picture than we can see or even begin to understand. Sometimes it is revealed to us as we look back; sometimes not. But God is *always* in control.

Is there a barren, dry area of your life that you would like God to transform? Is there an area where you are struggling, and you long for Him to turn your barren wilderness into a place of true joy and laughter? Offer that issue to Him now, in faith that He can make 'the wilderness... rejoice and blossom' (Isa. 35:1). Bear in mind, though, that it might not look like what you are imagining or are expecting. Our God is always full of surprises!

Genesis 17:19; 18:12; 21:1–7

'God has brought me laughter' (v6)

For prayer and reflection

Lord God, today I give You this area of my life where I've been struggling... I surrender it to You, and I ask You to transform my sadness into joy. Amen.

On **whose shoulders?**

Genesis 21:1–13

'Do not be so distressed… Listen to whatever Sarah tells you' (v12)

A braham is in a quandary. God has made it clear that Isaac is the child of His promise and the one through whom the covenant will be fulfilled. Yet Ishmael is Abraham's son too, and Abraham loves him.

When Sarah sees Ishmael interacting with Isaac, still a toddler, she sees red. Ishmael might just have been playing with him, or he might have been mocking him: we don't know – either translation of the Hebrew is valid. She tells Abraham to get rid of both him and Hagar, his mother. Clearly jealous, she wants to protect her own son's inheritance. Once again, Sarah struggles to trust God to bring about His purposes, and decides to interfere.

By getting rid of Hagar and Ishmael, Abraham would be disinheriting Ishmael. We are told in verse 11 that Abraham is very distressed by all this, and presumably doesn't know how to resolve the situation. We know Abraham just wants a simple life, and often looks for what appear to be the easiest solutions to his problems. As problems go, this is a biggie. How will he resolve it and keep everyone happy?

Once again, God steps in. He tells Abraham that he can abide by Sarah's wishes and that He will look after Ishmael. And he reiterates the promise that Ishmael's descendants will also become a nation in their own right (v13).

We have a tendency at times to want to solve every problem and to keep everyone happy. Sometimes, however, we need to let go and trust it all to God. It's not easy, especially when it concerns those we love dearly, but we can be assured that, as much as we love them, God loves them even more than we do, and He won't let them go.

For prayer and reflection

Commit your loved ones to God today. Name them one by one, and entrust them into His loving care.

Next Issue

September
PRAYER
REBECCA LOWE

October
THERE IS ALWAYS ENOUGH
ABBY KING

In **September**, Rebecca Lowe looks deeper into the privilege and power of being in communication with our God.

In **October**, Abby King looks more deeply into the story of the feeding of the 5,000, and what we can take from it today.

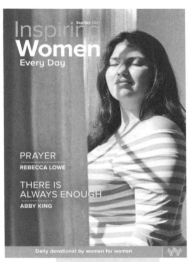

Available in a variety of formats

God sees, hears and provides

**Genesis
21:14–21**

'God heard the boy
crying, and the
angel of God
called to Hagar'
(v17)

I really can't help feeling sorry for Hagar in all of this. She didn't ask to be a slave; she was given no choice about sleeping with her mistress's husband or having a child on her behalf. And now she and her son are being driven away because of her mistress's insecurity and jealousy. They are victims of someone else's decisions and are suffering the consequences.

The food and water that Abraham sends with Hagar and Ishmael quickly runs out, and now, here in the desert, they are about to die of thirst. Hagar can't bear to watch her beloved son die, so she places him under a bush and walks away to weep bitterly.

Abraham and Sarah may have abandoned them, but God has not. He is faithful to His promise to Abraham to look after Hagar and Ishmael. He continues to 'see' them and to 'hear' them. In fact, the name Ishmael, which God told Hagar to give her son (Gen. 16:11), means 'God hears'. He calls to Hagar from heaven and reminds her of the promise He made to her, to make her son into a 'great nation'. Then He provides water for them. Presumably He provides food for them too, as Ishmael grows up in the desert (v20).

**For prayer
and reflection**

Father God, thank You that You see, You hear and You provide. Help me to be mindful of others in all the decisions I make. Amen.

The story of Abraham, Sarah and Hagar is a poignant reminder that we are all affected by other people's decisions – whether for good or for ill. We rail at the injustice of life sometimes, and complain that we are so hard done by. Yet we forget that other people are affected by our decisions too. And always, God is there: seeing, hearing and providing – for us and for those who might be affected by us and by the decisions we make.

Faithful **obedience**

Genesis 22:1–19

'Take your son,
your only son,
whom you love…
Sacrifice him' (v2)

Think for a moment – who, or what, is most precious to you in the whole world? Now imagine you have been asked to give it up. How does that make you feel? Not easy, is it? I think of my husband, my children, my family and friends. I couldn't even begin to imagine life without them.

Abraham is asked to sacrifice his beloved son, by the God who has given the child to him as a precious gift in the first place. Such a sacrifice to us is even more shocking than a slave bearing a child on behalf of her mistress.

Horrifically, child sacrifice wasn't unheard of in Abraham's time. The Canaanite god Molek was a deity to whom children would be sacrificed, to appease him. Needless to say, Yahweh, the God of Abraham, expressly forbids this practice (Lev. 18:21).

We can't even begin to imagine what might be going through Abraham's mind when he receives this instruction from God. Yet he obeys, without question. This demonstrates the utmost faith he has in God, that he is prepared to sacrifice the son by whom God has promised him countless descendants.

By preventing Abraham from sacrificing Isaac, God is making an important statement. He is clearly affirming that He is different from the gods of the people – He is not interested in child sacrifice; rather, He wants to save His people. Yahweh is a God of love, compassion and rescue.

When God provides the lamb for Abraham's sacrifice, there is a clear foreshadowing of the sacrifice of another Son, thousands of years later. Abraham's words in verse 8 are much truer than he realises: 'God himself will provide the lamb' (see also John 1:29,36).

**For prayer
and reflection**

**Abraham was
willing to sacrifice
everything for God.
How much am I
willing to sacrifice?
How much are
you?**

True loyalty

Genesis 22:1–19

'Through your offspring all nations on earth will be blessed, because you have obeyed me.' (v18)

Picture the scene. Abraham and Isaac are away for a few days, and Sarah is at home, managing the household and going about her regular, daily life. Her husband and son return, and Isaac comes bounding in to the tent. 'Mum, Mum! You'll never guess what happened…'

We can only imagine Sarah's reaction to hearing Isaac's news. 'Your dad was going to *what*?!'

Abraham, who, we have discovered, seems to desire an uncomplicated life, now has to defend himself to Sarah. How would his explanation go down – that God told him to sacrifice their precious boy, and then saved him at the last moment by providing a ram? What effect might this have on Abraham and Sarah's relationship? Would she share his trust in Yahweh and rejoice again at His promise, or would she struggle to trust her husband in future?

We don't know the answers to these questions, of course. But what we do know is that Abraham's loyalty, first and foremost, is to God. He's had his ups and downs, but it seems he has learnt that Yahweh is faithful and trustworthy, and deserves his complete obedience. As the vassal to Yahweh's suzerain in their covenant, perhaps Abraham is now finally learning what true loyalty and commitment really mean.

It isn't always easy to be obedient to God, especially when those around us don't share the vision we believe God has given us. Sometimes those closest to us don't share our faith, or find it hard to support what we believe God has asked us to do. Let's pray for the courage to be faithful and obedient, and to hear, discern and be obedient to God's voice over all the other voices in our lives.

For prayer and reflection

Father God, help me to hear Your voice over all others, and to be faithful and obedient to all that You are calling me to do in my life. Amen.

Foreshadowing

....

Luke 1:46–55

'merciful to Abraham and his descendants for ever, just as he promised our ancestors.' (vv54–55)

As we have seen over the last four weeks, Abraham and Sarah's story is just the beginning of God's incredible plan to restore humanity to relationship with Himself. When the angel Gabriel visits Mary to announce that she will have a child, and that that child will be none other than the Son of God Himself, the Messiah for whom the Jews have been waiting for hundreds of years, she is overwhelmed with joy and speaks these beautiful words about God's faithfulness throughout all the generations.

God's covenant and relationship with Abraham, as we have discovered, offer us a brief foresight of the New Covenant that Jesus will bring. The near-sacrifice of Isaac is a foreshadowing of the sacrifice of Jesus on the cross. Note how, in Genesis 22:6, Isaac himself carries the wood on which he is about to be sacrificed – shades of Jesus, the Lamb of God, carrying his own cross to Calvary (see John 19:17).

Take some time this weekend to meditate on Mary's song, verse by verse, and listen to what God wants to say to you through it.

....

Optional further reading

John 19; 1 Corinthians 11:23–26

A **difficult** life

Genesis 23:1–20

'Sarah lived to be a hundred and twenty-seven years old.' (v1)

Sarah didn't have an easy life. There were times when she probably felt worthless and unfulfilled, unable to have a child for so many years, and that she'd 'failed' in her duty to continue her husband's family line. She may have felt undervalued, when her husband twice passed her off as his sister rather than risk his own skin.

Sarah made mistakes. She and Abraham took matters into their own hands instead of trusting God. She gave in to jealousy and insecurity and gave no thought to the needs and feelings of Hagar, her slave.

Sarah wasn't perfect. Yet she played a huge part in God's plan for humanity. God chose her to bear the son through whom His covenant with Abraham would be fulfilled. He stepped in to save her and to deal with the consequences of her actions on more than one occasion.

I wonder what Sarah's thoughts might have been as she looked back on her life. Did she regret some of the mistakes she had made? Did she begin to see the bigger picture that God was painting, or would that only begin to become apparent with the benefit of hundreds of years of history?

Think about what we have discovered about Sarah this month. What has spoken to you most about her life? How do you think you might have responded to the various events in her life, had you been in her shoes? Would you have made similar mistakes, or might you have done things differently?

How have you seen God transform some of the challenging situations in your life? Can you think of any times when He has brought to fruition His plans in spite of any mistakes you might have made?

For prayer and reflection

Thank You, Lord, that Your plans are far bigger than any mistakes I might make in my life. May Your will and Your plans always come to pass. Amen.

God's promise **continues**

E ach of us plays but a small part in God's great plan for humanity. Abraham's part was, arguably, more memorable than many, but we are all called to do our bit. God has placed each of us where we are for a reason – in our family, in our workplace, in our neighbourhood, in our friendship groups.

Genesis 25:1–11

'After Abraham's death, God blessed his son Isaac' (v11)

And God's plan is far bigger than each of us individually, and infinitely greater than we could ever begin to understand. Abraham didn't see the fulfilment of the majority of the promises God made to him, but Abraham 'believed the LORD, and he credited it to him as righteousness' (Gen. 15:6).

Abraham waited many years for God's promise of a son to be fulfilled. He made some mistakes along the way, but God remained faithful to His promises and plans. And Abraham died in faith that the fulfilment of the rest of God's promise was still to come.

Is there a promise that you are still waiting for God to fulfil in your life? Ask Him for the patience to wait, and to trust in His perfect timing. We don't always understand God's plans – and we don't necessarily need to. We simply need to trust and obey, just as Abraham learned to do.

As we reflect on the lives of Abraham and Sarah and their part in God's big story, think about the part that God has called you to play. How has God gifted you to play that part? Who are the people God has put in your life to witness to? How can you bring God's kingdom to the people around you?

I have greatly enjoyed journeying with Abraham and Sarah this month, and I have learnt so much from their lives. I hope and pray that it has been a blessing for you too.

For prayer and reflection

God of Abraham, Isaac and Jacob, thank You for Your plan to save human beings from our sin. Help me to play my part in Your plan for this world. Amen.

Notes

Order form

Get Your **FREE** Daily Bible Reading Notes **TODAY! (UK ONLY)**

Your favourite Bible reading notes are now FREE. God has called us back to the original vision of CWR to provide these notes to everyone who needs them, regardless of their circumstance or ability to pay. It is our desire to see these daily Bible reading notes used more widely, to see Christians grow in their relationship with Jesus on a daily basis and to see Him reflected in their everyday living. Clearly there are costs to provide this ministry and we are trusting in God's provision.

Could you be part of this vision? Do you have the desire to see lives transformed through a relationship with Jesus? **A small donation from you of just £2 a month, by direct debit, will make such a difference** Giving hope to someone in desperate need whilst you too grow deeper in your own relationship with Jesus.

4 Easy Ways To Order

1. Visit our online store at **waverleyabbeyresources.org/store**
2. Send this form together with your payment to: **CWR, Waverley Abbey House, Waverley Lane, Farnham, Surrey GU9 8EP**
3. Phone in your credit card order: **01252 784700** (Mon–Fri, 9.30am – 4.30pm)
4. Visit a Christian bookshop

For a list of our National Distributors, who supply countries outside the UK, visit waverleyabbeyresources.org/distributors

Your Details (required for orders and donations)

Full Name:		CWR ID No. (if known):
Home Address:		
		Postcode:
Telephone No. (for queries):		Email:

Publications

TITLE	QTY	PRICE	TOTAL
		TOTAL PUBLICATIONS	

UK P&P: up to £24.99 = **£2.99**; £25.00 and over = **FREE**

Elsewhere P&P: up to £10 = **£4.95**; £10.01 – £50 = **£6.95**; £50.01 – £99.99 = **£10**; £100 and over = **£30**

Total Publications and P&P (please allow 14 days for delivery)	**A**	

Payment Details

☐ I enclose a cheque made payable to CWR for the amount of: **£** _____

☐ Please charge my credit/debit card.

Cardholder's Name (in BLOCK CAPITALS) _____

Card No. ☐☐☐☐ ☐☐☐☐ ☐☐☐☐ ☐☐☐☐ ☐☐☐☐

Expires End ☐☐☐☐   Security Code ☐☐☐

Continued overleaf >>

<< See previous page for start of order form

| **One off Special Gift to CWR** | ☐ Please send me an acknowledgement of my gift **B** | |

GRAND TOTAL (Total of A & B)

Gift Aid (your home address required, see overleaf)

giftaid it I am a UK taxpayer and want CWR to reclaim the tax on all my donations for the four years prior to this year **and on** all donations I make from the date of this Gift Aid declaration until further notice.*

Taxpayer's Full Name (in BLOCK CAPITALS) _____

Signature _____ **Date** _____

*I am a UK taxpayer and understand that if I pay less Income Tax and/or Capital Gains Tax than the amount of Gift Aid claimed on all my donations in that tax year it is my responsibility to pay any difference.

Your FREE Daily Bible Reading Notes Order

	Please Tick	FREE	£2 pcm	£5 pcm	£10 pcm	Other
Every Day with Jesus		☐	☐	☐	☐	☐ £ _____
Large Print *Every Day with Jesus*		☐	☐	☐	☐	☐ £ _____
Inspiring Women Every Day		☐	☐	☐	☐	☐ £ _____

All CWR Bible reading notes are also available in single issue **ebook** and **email subscription** format. Visit **waverleyabbeyresources.org** for further info.

CWR Instruction to your Bank or Building Society to pay by Direct Debit

DIRECT Debit

Please fill in the form and send to: CWR, Waverley Abbey House,
Waverley Lane, Farnham, Surrey GU9 8EP

Name and full postal address of your Bank or Building Society

To: The Manager   Bank/Building Society

Address

_____

_____

_____ Postcode

Name(s) of Account Holder(s)

Branch Sort Code

Bank/Building Society Account Number

Originator's Identification Number

| 4 | 2 | 0 | 4 | 8 | 7 |

Reference

Instruction to your Bank or Building Society

Please pay CWR Direct Debits from the account detailed in this Instruction subject to the safeguards assured by the Direct Debit Guarantee. I understand that this Instruction may remain with CWR and, if so, details will be passed electronically to my Bank/Building Society.

Signature(s)

_____

_____

Date

Banks and Building Societies may not accept Direct Debit Instructions for some types of account

---

For a subscription outside of the UK please visit www.waverleyabbeyresources.org where you will find a list of our national distributors.

How would you like to hear from us? We would love to keep you up to date on all aspects of the CWR ministry, including; new publications, events & courses as well as how you can support us.

If you **DO** want to hear from us on email, please tick here [ ] If you **DO NOT** want us to contact you by post, please tick here [ ]
You can update your preferences at any time by contacting our customer services team on 01252 784 700. You can view our privacy policy online at waverleyabbeyresources.org